This book belongs to

____

Happiness
IS A CUP OF
COFFEE
& A GOOD
Book

DRINK
COFFEE
AND
DO
Good

Coffee
IS
ALWAYS -
A GOOD
Idea

A COFFEE
A DAY
KEEP THE
GRUMPY
AWAY

Good
Coffee
Good Day

Good
Morning
Starts
·WITH·
COFFEE

This will
ALL
MAKE SENSE
AFTER
COFFEE

IT'S
Always
COFFEE
Time

Life
Begins
AFTER
COFFEE

Wake Up and Smell the Coffee

FIRST
I DRINK
coffee
THEN
I DO THE
Things

May
your
coffee
kickin
Before
the reality
Does

STRESSED

blessed

and

coffee

obsessed

MAY YOUR Coffee BE STRONG AND YOUR MONDAY be short

COFFEE
IS MY
SPIRIT
Animal

WAKE UP
AND
SMELL
THE
COFFEE

GOOD
Vibes
AND
GOOD
Coffee

Love
is in
THE AIR
AND
it smells like
COFFEE

In Coffee We Trust

Coffee
IS MY
BEST
Friend

Make
SOMEONE
HAPPY
-WITH A-
Coffee

IT'S
COFFEE
O'CLOCK

I Want
Coffee
not
your
OPINION

Hocus Pocus I need coffee to focus

All we need
is
a CUP of
morning
Coffee

Start
your
class
with
coffee

Coffee
And Then The
World

COFFEE IS LIKE A HUG IN A MUG

COFFEE
MAKES
EVERYTHING
BETTER

COFFEE IS THE MOST IMPORTANT MEAL OF THE DAY

TODAY'S GOOD MORNING IS SPONSORED BY COFFEE

THE
Aroma
OF COFFEE
Is The
Aroma
OF LIFE

LIFE
happens
COFFEE
helps

Share your lovely coloring
work with us:

Twitter @BeakyStarlight
Facebook @BeakyAndStarlight

Produced by Beaky and Starlight Ltd.

Published : March 2021

ISBN:9798715207418

For more information about the publisher, please visit:

www.facebook.com/BeakyAndStarlight/